J
751.4

Hodge, Anthony
Painting

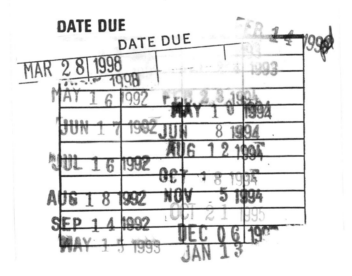

© Aladdin Books 1991

*First published in 1991
in the United States by*
Gloucester Press
387 Park Avenue South
New York, NY 10016

Library of Congress Cataloging-in-Publication Data

Hodge, Anthony.
    Painting / Anthony Hodge.
        p.   cm. -- (Hands on arts and crafts)
    Includes index.
    Summary: Introduces portraiture, still life, landscape painting,
abstract painting, and surrealism; demonstrates painting techniques,
and includes examples of author's paintings.
    ISBN 0-531-17299-6
    1. Painting--Techniques--Juvenile literature. [1. Painting-
-Technique. 2. Art appreciation.] I. Series.
ND1146.H6   1991
751.4--dc20   90-45004   CIP   AC

Printed in Belgium

The author, Anthony Hodge, is an artist
whose work is regularly exhibited. He has
taught art to adults and children for 20
years.

Design: Rob Hillier, Andy Wilkinson
Editor: Jen Green
Paintings by Anthony Hodge
Illustrations by Ron Hayward Associates

HANDS ON ARTS AND CRAFTS

PAINTING

Anthony Hodge

Gloucester Press
New York · London · Toronto · Sydney

CONTENTS

INTRODUCTION

"An artist is not a special kind of person, but every person is a special kind of artist." A. Coomaraswamy, writer and artist.

This book provides an introduction to a series of ideas and techniques that will help you express yourself in paint. Painting is an area in which everyone can be of equal value, because each person's work is unique. Some of you have an eye for detail; others form a general impression of the world. These differences will be reflected in how you paint.

Freedom to experiment
The projects in this book cover a wide range of different kinds of painting. One project leads on to the next. We will start with tools and materials, color-mixing and other practical skills. Later a series of projects will introduce ways of using these techniques, bringing in your own ideas.

What you need
Before you begin, you will need to be wearing old clothes which may get splashed with paint. You will also need newspaper or an old sheet to cover the surface on which you work, and somewhere to put your work while it dries. Clean your brushes thoroughly with water when you finish using them. If you use oil paint, you will need turpentine and rags, followed by soap and water, to clean your brushes when you finish.

△ *"Here is a detail from a seascape I painted at Newlyn Harbor in Cornwall, England. Even when you paint from life, it's important to feel free to experiment and bring in ideas from your imagination.*

If an impulse comes to you, go along with it and see where it leads you. Some of the best ideas arrive from nowhere, so keep an open mind, relax and above all, be sure to enjoy yourself."

TOOLS AND MATERIALS

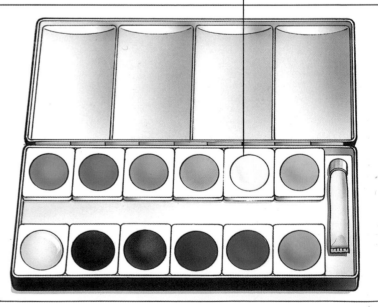

Most paintings are done with brushes, but there are many other ways paint can be applied. In the picture you can see a few examples and you may be able to think of more. Make a collection of brushes and other mark-making implements and get ready for an experimental session with them.

A good palette is an especially important tool, to mix your colors on. It must be large enough to carry plenty of paint, and have room left over for unexpected extra color-mixing. A wooden palette from the art supply store is a good investment, as it is seasoned wood and can be cleaned easily. Otherwise plastic or another nonabsorbent surface will do.

Poster paint is a cheap form of gouache. It comes in pots or paint boxes. Make sure you get plenty of color on your brushes.

Which paint suits you best?

Colors are made of *pigments* (colored powders), most of which are mined from the ground and mixed with various binding materials to perform different jobs. You may find one kind of paint or *medium* suits you so well that you use it all the time, or you may like to keep changing from one to another. Other kinds of paints not featured here are emulsion, tempera and gloss.

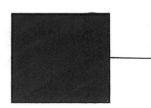

Acrylic is a paint made of plastic. It can be used thin like watercolor or thick like oil. It dries quickly, so don't squeeze out too much.

Surfaces to paint on

The paintings in this book are mostly in acrylic on white paper or cardboard. Acrylic can be used on most things. Oil paint will sink into most surfaces if they haven't been prepared with a *primer* like gesso or size. Try using oil on hardboard, canvas, cardboard and plywood; get off-cuts from local stores. Don't spend all your money in the art supply store – expensive equipment can stop you working in a relaxed way.

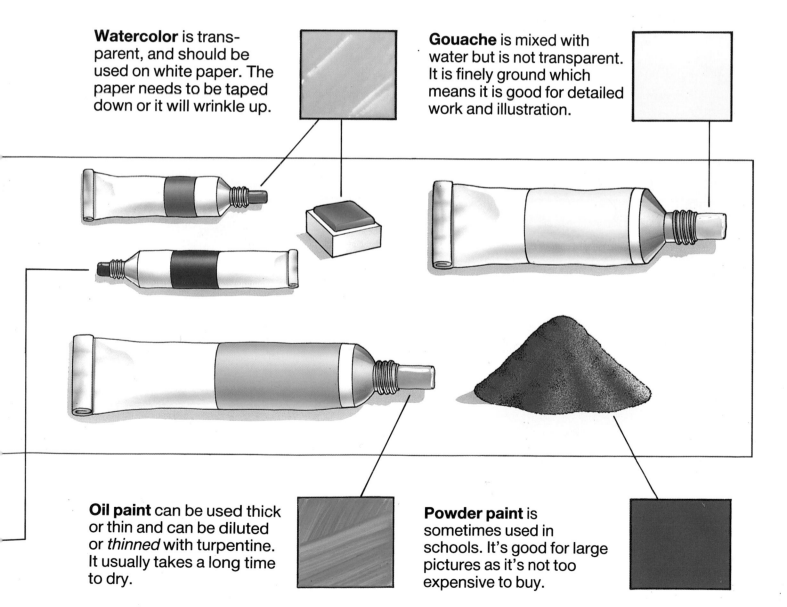

Watercolor is transparent, and should be used on white paper. The paper needs to be taped down or it will wrinkle up.

Gouache is mixed with water but is not transparent. It is finely ground which means it is good for detailed work and illustration.

Oil paint can be used thick or thin and can be diluted or *thinned* with turpentine. It usually takes a long time to dry.

Powder paint is sometimes used in schools. It's good for large pictures as it's not too expensive to buy.

FEELING YOUR WAY

An important part of painting is allowing yourself to enjoy the materials. The main aim of this project is to see what they can do rather than what you can do. Try to relax and watch what happens with interest, rather than being too critical of yourself. You will need a large piece of paper and the paints, brushes and other mark-making tools you gathered earlier.

An exercise in mark-making
The project is to make as many kinds of marks as you can. With different tools you can make blobs, smears, draggings, squiggles, patches, anything. The painting on the opposite page shows a sponge print, lines straight from the tube, a line with a square-ended brush, a finger, a palette knife smear, a big brush stroke and stipple, and a toothbrush flick.

On your marks
The marks you make will sometimes accidentally look like "real" things. Some tools are good for creating leaves, others for cat's fur, clouds and so on. The marks in these examples look like foliage, grass and flowers. When you have filled a page with different marks, pick out the ones that remind you of real things and then make them part of a separate painting of your own, using appropriate colors.

It also includes a trail, made by letting the paint run by picking the paper up and turning it, and two sable brush lines (the brush was turned to get both thick and thin lines). Can you tell which is which?

Slow or speedy?

The kind of paint used here is acrylic, but use whatever you have or try several kinds of paint together.

Don't try and make a "real" picture but spend time noticing the different effects you can produce. At this stage the marks don't "mean" anything, but you will notice that some look speedy and others slow. Some are soft, others look rough and crude. Notice how different tools, for example, a soft brush or a hard knife, make the paint behave in very different ways.

△ *"Above is a variety of marks I made using colors at random and as many different tools as I could find. After you* have experimented with this, choose colors to suit particular kinds of marks, or try the whole project in one color."

7

PURE COLOR

This project is to give you a chance to get to know the colors in your tubes or paintbox and to practice using them *flat*, in their pure form, without mixing them together.

If you look around you, you will see all kinds of colors, some bright, some dull, some easy to name, and some neither one nor the other. The world can look very complicated when you start trying to paint it. Some painters avoid looking at real things and just make things up! But most people like to paint what they see, at least from time to time.

Choosing your subject

Make a collection of everyday objects that correspond as closely as possible with the six pure colors from the color wheel (bottom right). Don't forget to include something to use as background – a bright curtain, perhaps, or a piece of colored paper. Find something red, blue, green, yellow, orange and purple. Take some time arranging everything in a group so that you can see all the objects clearly and they aren't in each other's way. Your painting will turn out very bright and cheerful.

8

You may like the bright colors so much that in future you may paint things brighter than they really are. Keep the colors clean when painting by using a different brush for each new color or by making sure you clean your brushes thoroughly between colors.

▽ *"For the painting below I first made a simple drawing in pencil. I spent some time deciding where the colors would go. You can see that some of the marks look a bit like the ones I made on the previous page. Paint several pictures of this subject and choose the one you like best."*

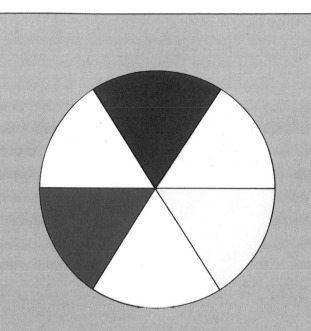

Primary colors
Here are the three basic or *primary* colors and their position on what is called the "color wheel." There are many kinds of red, yellow and blue but the primaries are the purest you can get.

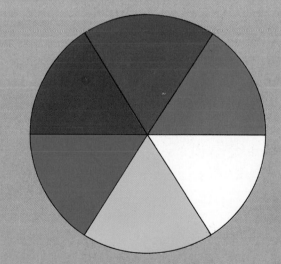

Secondary colors
Here are the primaries again with their neighbors: orange, green and purple. These are the *secondary* colors, mixed from the two primaries on either side of them. Experiment with painting the color wheel yourself.

9

MIXING COLORS

The pure colors used on the previous page can be put into pairs of opposites or *complementaries*. These are red and green, yellow and purple, and blue and orange. You can see them opposite each other on the color wheel. Black and white are also opposites and will be dealt with more fully below and on page 13. Some pictures are painted entirely with two complementaries, creating other colors by mixing them in different ways. Landscapes are often made of red and green, and these are the two colors used in the picture opposite, mixed with white in places.

Landscapes in pairs of colors

In the fall, when the sky is often clear and the leaves are bright, or in spring, with new life growing, other pairs of colors may be more appropriate. Winter could be seen as black and white. See if you can think of other subjects that would suit a particular pair of complementaries. Every color, however subtle, has its own complementary.

Paint a simple landscape in a pair of complementaries mixed with white. You may be surprised to discover that you don't need many colors to paint an interesting and atmospheric picture. Use different kinds of brushwork, thick and thin, fast and slow, for different effects.

Inside or out?

If you enjoy painting from life, go out looking for a subject or just paint the view from your window. On the other hand, you may prefer painting a place you know from memory, or just making something up. Whichever you choose, begin painting by mixing some colors on the palette, keeping them fresh and separate.

▷ *"In the painting on the right I have used pure color in the foreground (the part of the picture that looks nearest to the viewer), and mixes of red and green for the foliage and tree trunks beyond. For the sky, road and the grass in the distance I have added white. I made a pencil sketch first, then mixed my colors and began."*

White has the effect of making colors both lighter and less bright. With the exception of watercolors, all mediums use white to increase subtlety, but overuse can make your pictures look chalky and washed out. With watercolor, subtlety is obtained by using varying amounts of water to dilute the color. When you surround white with a pure color, it will appear to be tinged with the complementary of the pure color. Try it and see.

Pairs of opposites

Colors mixed with white become more subtle, as shown in the top left corner of each color square. When mixed together, complementary colors make grey, as shown in the bottom right corners. Painted side by side, opposite colors enhance or bring out the best in each other.

BRIGHTNESS, TONE AND HUE

Learning about colors is a bit like learning to speak a different language. If the first few pages of this book seem like hard work, think of them as needing to learn a new vocabulary so that you can express yourself with confidence in future.

All colors have three qualities
These qualities are brightness, tone and hue. The brightness or dullness of a color compares with a loud or soft note in music. Tone means how light or dark a color is when compared to another color. A note in music has an equivalent high or low sound. Lastly, each color also has a hue, which is equivalent to the actual note in music. The hue is the actual color you are left with when

Playing scales in color
Brightness, tone and hue are illustrated in the color charts on the right. The top one demonstrates a progression of brightness to dullness, the middle shows light to dark tones, and the bottom one is a progression of the color pink to green in the same tone and brightness, to demonstrate hue. If colors of the same tone and brightness are placed side by side, as shown below, they seem to shimmer and dance together in front of your eyes. It is difficult to get this right, but if you learn to recognize when it *is* right you are beginning to get some real control with color-mixing.

differences in tone and brightness have been removed.

Seeing hue

The idea of this project is to make a picture in which all the colors are the same tone and as much as possible the same brightness. What you will then see is their hue. Choose some colors; experiment with mixing them and painting them in simple patches. The patches below have been made into buildings. First mix your colors. Look at them on the palette and change them around until they are all the same tone before you start painting. Use black to darken or quiet colors if they look too light or too bright. Try to keep the colors clean and flat.

◁ *"To keep colors on separate brushes clean, I stand the brushes bristles up in a can with holes punched in the lid. Alternatively, you could use a container filled with scrunched-up chicken wire."*

Black is introduced here as a way of making colors darker in tone and less bright. It can also be used as a color in its own right. Like white, it may appear to be affected by colors that surround it. Sometimes painters use lines of black to separate the colors in their pictures, as panes of colored glass are separated. This can have the effect of bringing order to a chaotic image.

13

MAKING IT LOOK "REAL"

Two painters once had a competition to see who could paint the most realistic picture. The pictures were to be unveiled to the judges. The first drew back the curtains. His picture was of fruit in a bowl. Birds came and pecked at it. Everyone was very impressed. The second painter was asked to draw back his curtains to reveal his picture. He replied that they were already looking at it. He had painted a pair of curtains.

Painting in 3-D

There is always a special kind of thrill in making something you paint look real. We all know the world is made up of solid things we can pick up or walk around. But the surface of a painting, board or piece of paper is flat. If you are painting an apple, how can you make it look fresh and good enough to eat?

One way to make your pictures look solid is to examine how light falls on the subject. As the sun moves across the sky and the shadows come and go, the appearance of your subject can change very much. The world changes constantly in front of you as you try to capture it, especially outside on a sunny day.

Careful observation

Find a simply colored object, an apple or an orange perhaps.

Look carefully at how its hues, tones and brightness change as you move it around. Look at it closely, get to know the apple in all lights, and familiarize yourself with its shape and colors. Try placing the apple so that the light comes strongly from one direction. Paint the apple in your mind's eye before you begin. Then make three paintings, each showing a different effect of light.

▽ *"My examples below show the same apple in three different lights. Notice how my colors become gradually darker and bluer as the shadows deepen. Make your picture life-size or larger, so you can really show what's happening without getting bogged down in small details."*

Changing light

The diagrams below show the effects of light shined on a round form from a number of different directions (indicated by the arrows). Reproducing this effect will involve the technique of blending colors. As the light changes to shadow, so colors change accordingly. You might practice these changes on a separate piece of paper before beginning your painting. Some painters feel that the shadow of an object can be represented by the complementary of the color that is in the light. Do your observations bear this out?

15

PORTRAITS

"Why can't you be more like an apple!" Cezanne used to shout at people he was painting. A head may be a bit like an apple but a face has expressions and doesn't find it easy to stay still and always look the same.

Beginning work
The project here is to paint a portrait. Ask someone to pose for you who won't mind whether your picture is like them or not. Grandparents can be ideal. Make sure that your subject is comfortable and relaxed. Alternatively, paint with a friend, working on one another's portraits.

Step by step
Take time to have a good look at your subject. Then begin by drawing in pencil, and then with very thin paint, the simple shape of the face. Mark in the lines for the features as shown in the diagram below. Lightly lay in the eyes, ears, nose, mouth and hair. Have a good look at the color of your model's skin, hair and clothes, and the color of the background.

Setting the mood
Mix up the main colors you need. Remember that they, as much as anything else, will give the picture its mood. Adjust them until you are satisfied with your basic ingredients. Then paint them down as flat areas of color. Give your portrait depth and solidity by modeling highlights and shadows over the flat colors.

▷ *"My examples show the four stages described above. Light is shining on the face from one side, and I have introduced light and shadow areas accordingly. Don't be afraid of changing your picture as you go along. The character of your subject may only become clear gradually. It's important not to put in too many details at an early stage, for you may be reluctant to paint over them even if you should."*

Proportions of the head
The drawing near right shows the average proportions of the head. One thing that may surprise you is that the eyes come halfway down the head and not higher up, as you might suppose. The lower part is divided in half again where the nose ends, and in half again at the mouth. The second picture shows the proportions of the same head in *profile*, from a side view.

△ Misery
▽ Peacefulness

Mood, shape and color

There are no strict rules linking colors with particular feelings. Blue is usually thought of as sad but it can also be peaceful; orange can be cheerful but also angry. Yellow can be warm like the sun, but quite the opposite as the color of someone's face. It all depends on how color is used.

Shape can also express mood and emotion. A triangle sits firmly on the ground and might convey stability, or hope. A rectangle may also seem calm, or it might feel restrictive. A circle seems likely to move or float; it might convey a sense of completeness or of isolation. A star explodes with vitality, and seems to grow bigger as you look at it. Which colors fit best with each of these shapes?

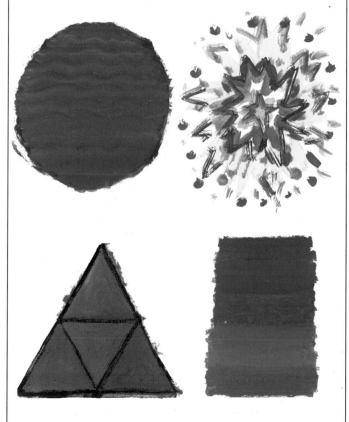

EXPRESSING YOURSELF

Painters paint self-portraits for all kinds of reasons, but the most obvious has to be that your own face is always there when you want it. Have a good look in the mirror and see what shape yours is. Ask yourself what kind of person you are and how you can show this in a painting. Are you cheerful or sad? Do you shout a lot or do you keep things bottled up? Do you like to do things quickly, or do you take your time? Using some of the ideas from the previous projects, try to combine careful observation and the expression of feeling in a portrait of yourself.

Getting set up

Begin by getting comfortable. Place your paper or board on an easel or rest it against a wall or the back of a chair. Arrange yourself in such a way that you can look straight from the mirror to your painting without turning your head too much.

Make a pencil sketch as you did earlier, taking care to establish the particular proportions of your face. Mix your colors, and change them around until you are satisfied that they represent you.

Showing how you feel

Do several pictures of yourself in different moods and change the colors and the way you put on the paint accordingly. After the first painting, you may want to dispense with the mirror and paint your "inner self" from imagination.

△ *"These three portraits use color to convey mood. This boy in shades of pink looks gentle and thoughtful."*

Features and expressions

Here are examples of the same face with three very different expressions, looking in turn angry, frightened and perplexed. These emotions are conveyed chiefly through the shape of the mouth and eyes. Notice, however, that the eyebrows, hair, even the nose and ears can also express emotion. Lines and shapes turning upward look cheerful and full of life; turning down they look sad or fierce. To convey perplexity the lines are undecided and may turn in both directions.

△ *"I have tried to convey the scattiness and good humor of this boy through the use of bright colors and jagged strokes."*

△ *"My third sitter seemed anxious and sad. I chose gloomy colors and applied them with nervous, scratchy strokes."*

IMAGINATION

Imagination means image-making. With it you can create pictures of things that in real life could never happen (or not very often anyway). Through painting you can create a world which is strange, magical, shocking or just plain crazy.

Unusual combinations

The project here is to base a painting on the idea of combining two unrelated subjects. When these come together they make something new with a separate life of its own. The illustration near right shows a man and a tree. In the painting opposite, the same words came together to make a tree-man. If you look in the background you will see a man-tree as an alternative.

Seeing pictures in your head

One way of getting ideas for a painting of this kind is to write down lots of ideas on separate pieces of paper and put them in a bag.

Pick pairs of them at random out of the bag. When you see two words together, what picture, if any, comes into your mind of how they could be joined? Keep trying different combinations. Practice seeing as much detail as possible in your mind's eye before starting to paint.

▷ *"My tree-man picture is painted with a big brush for the trees and sky and a smaller one for the head and hands. The brush marks in the foreground and in the foliage look like grass and leaves."*

Changing step by step

The idea of putting together two things and making a third can be a starting point for all kinds of ideas. Opposite you can see how a man changing into a tiger might work step by step. This process is called transformation or metamorphosis. Perhaps you can imagine how a similar sequence happened while the man was changing into a tree, which the main picture shows halfway through. How would it look at an earlier or later stage in the process of transformation?

There are many other ways of using your imagination. Dreams provide images that can become powerful paintings – can you remember any of yours? Daydreaming can also make amazing and wonderful things come true. A wolf hatching from an egg? A fossilized car?

COMPOSITION

Composition is another word whose meaning is hard to pin down. Literally it means putting things together. If you take the ingredients for a cake one by one and taste them separately, it is not the same as tasting the cake itself. In the same way your picture is made up of different ingredients that come together to form a new whole. Within it, colored shapes and light and dark areas have to work together. Each part must be in place and not demand your attention so much that you can't see the picture as a single thing.

Try it yourself
A good way to practice composition is by using colored paper which can be cut or torn to the shape you want. By moving your pieces of paper around, you can experiment to achieve a sense of unity before you finally glue them down.

Ripping off ideas
A good subject for this technique, called collage, is people in action. Look through newspapers or magazines to find a photograph that appeals to you for your subject. Then compose your own collage based loosely on the photograph. Don't glue anything down until you have tried your ingredients in a number of different positions first.

▷ *"My composition is basically triangular. Your eyes climb up to the ball as the soccer players do. Some of the colored pieces for the arms and legs don't look very real on their own, but they play their part in the whole."*

A journey around your picture
Compositions are often based on simple shapes like a triangle, a circle or a spiral. Having first seen the whole image, your eyes then follow the movement of the composition. In the team picture your eyes can either look along the rows of heads or move in a zigzag between them. What happens when you look at the runners below? Always try to give your eyes an exciting journey.

PERSPECTIVE

Perspective, which means "looking through," is a way of creating the illusion of three-dimensional space on the flat surface of a picture. The kind of perspective that is usually most familiar is based on the idea that the painting on the wall is like a window through which we can see the real world.

Getting angles right

Everyone knows how difficult it can sometimes be to get a particular angle of a building or table exactly right, so that it looks as if it were moving toward or away from us. People who find this skill difficult to master often give up the idea of being good at art before they have discovered all the

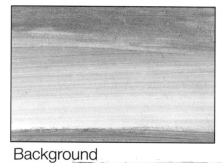
Background

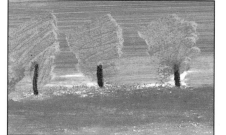
Middle ground

Foreground

other aspects of painting that are exciting and enjoyable.

Creating distance

There are at least four different ways of showing that one thing is behind or in front of another. Many pictures combine several or all four, though some use none at all.

◁ *"The sky in my picture opposite shows that a strong blue can appear to be in front of a paler, thinner blue as it fades toward the horizon. I used the brightest colors in the foreground and middle distance. I applied the paint thickly and more vigorously in those areas too."*

For the painter perhaps the most appropriate way of portraying distance is through color. As a rule, dark and dull colors tend to go back, or recede, in space. Light and bright ones tend to come forward. Think of how the rays of a yellow sun reach out from a background of blue sky.

The strongest contrasts in tone should be in the foreground. Colors in a landscape seem to get bluer and mistier the further away they are, and the same effect can be achieved in painting. Recession can also be emphasized by using thinner paint in the middle and background. Paint a landscape and test out these theories.

A sense of space

The diagrams below illustrate some of the other ways of showing perspective. The first is an example of "linear" or line perspective. Lines that would in fact run parallel in the real world, like the roadsides in the diagram, appear to meet at a point on the horizon called the "vanishing point."

The second diagram shows an example of overlapping. The hill that blocks out part of another hill must be in front of it; the human figure blocks them all out and so must be the nearest thing to you. In the third diagram the darker, stronger and "speedier" lines and tones in the foreground appear to be in front of the softer, "slower" lines.

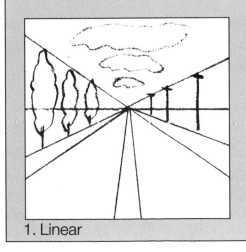

1. Linear

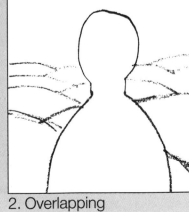

2. Overlapping

3. Tonal

DIFFERENT WAYS OF SEEING

Long ago ancient civilizations had very different ways of viewing the world than we in the West are familiar with today. Persian, Indian, Egyptian and Chinese cultures all evolved artistic traditions that reflected their own outlooks. For some of them the idea was not to show what a scene looked like from any one place or at one time, but to represent their subject from a number of viewpoints at once, or at a number of different times simultaneously.

Seeing the world as flat
Many modern painters have placed a similar importance on the picture as a flat pattern in which every part is of equal value. In their work, colors and shapes sit side by side on the surface of the picture, as they do in the main painting below, rather than trying to fool the eye and create the illusion of space, as shown in the watercolor below left.

Seeing from many angles
Try this approach with a painting of your own room at home. This project is not about standing on one spot, gazing ahead and painting what you see with mathematical precision. Walk around your room instead and decide which viewpoint is best for each of the objects you want to include. You could also put yourself in the picture.

▽ *"Below is a room I have painted from a single viewpoint with linear perspective. The space in the room is defined by receding lines which make the front look bigger and the rear smaller."*

▷ *"My painting on the right involves a number of different viewpoints. The table-top is seen from above, the vase from the side, while the fruit bowl is a bit of both."*

Through Egyptian eyes

A striking example of multiviewpoint is found in the art of the ancient Egyptians, whose style of painting remained almost unchanged for 5,000 years. Egyptian tradition demanded the representation of certain things from particular angles, regardless of whether it was possible to see these angles simultaneously in the real world. Artists felt that this method would best express the essence of their subject. A face, for example, should be shown from the side, whereas an eye was most like an eye when seen from the front. This method produced an idealization rather than a copy of the world.

PRESENTATION

Your work will always look better when it is put into a mat or a frame and hung on a wall. Pictures need to be separated from everyday life to be seen properly. Looking over your work over a period of time will also help you to see it as a separate thing.

Reworking

You may notice things you want to change. Sometimes you may find that there are parts that you don't like: for example, a color may appear too bright or too dull. Reworking should be approached with caution. If your picture is free and spontaneous, you may spoil it by overpainting.

When to stop

Judging the right moment to stop is an important skill to develop. When that decision is made, the painting has reached the end of its journey and must be able to stand by itself.

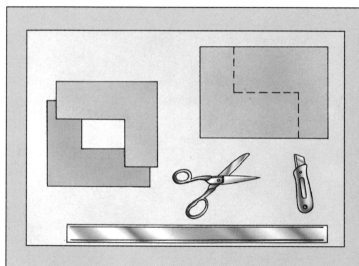

Selecting your image

If your painting does not seem to work satisfactorily as it is, part of it may. Selecting which part to use can be fascinating. By cutting out a pair of L-shapes as shown in the diagram above, you can isolate a portion that may look more appealing on its own. By moving the L-shapes over the surface of the picture, you can change the size and shape of your composition very easily. Then by measuring the space within the L-shapes you can find out the dimensions for your mat.

Mounting your work

When you have decided on your final composition, cut a mat to display it. Mats should be cut equally on both sides, but make sure your mat is wider at the bottom than at the top, as shown in the middle mat below. Otherwise when it is hanging the mat will look unbalanced.

A pale gray or cream mat is right for many pictures, but sometimes colored mats can be effective. Choose a color that brings out the mood or the colors of the picture. On the whole, avoid very brightly colored mats, as they will tend to draw attention away from your actual painting.

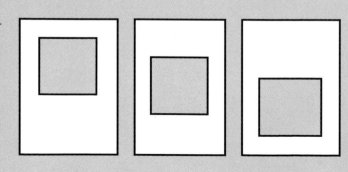

PRACTICAL TIPS

Your starting kit

Before you begin painting, you will need a starting kit of basic equipment. Whichever **paint** you choose, you will need at least five colors – start with cadmium red, cadmium yellow, ultramarine (blue), white and black. Add yellow ochre, viridian (green), burnt umber and cobalt blue if you can.

Many kinds of **brushes** are available, suitable for different kinds of paint. Brushes are numbered according to size. You will need at least three brushes to begin with: a thick and a thin coarse brush, and a fine brush for details. Brush prices vary greatly; more expensive ones will probably last longer and produce better results.

A **palette knife** can be used to apply oil or acrylic paint, to produce hard, flat marks or to build up layers of paint. For a **palette** you could use an old plate (a white one is best) or tin lid. For water-soluble paints you will need jelly jars to hold water and for oil or acrylic paint a **dipper** or some small containers for your thinners (discussed below).

Preparing your surface

Before you use oil or acrylic paint you will need to *prime* your surface, unless you are using a prepared canvas. For acrylic paint use a special acrylic primer. For oil paint, give your surface a coat of primer such as size or gesso, using a household paint brush.

Stretching your paper will be necessary if you use water-soluble paint. Immerse your paper in water so that both sides are thoroughly wet.

Place it on a flat board, and smooth out the creases with a sponge. Tape it to the board with brown paper tape, and let it dry. Leave your paper taped to the board while you paint. Later, if you remove the tape with your finished painting, it will fit well under a mat.

Adding thinners

Paint is usually *thinned*, or diluted, but the thinner that should be used varies with the kind of paint. Water-soluble paints like watercolors, gouache, powder and poster paint are diluted with water. Oil paint is thinned with linseed oil and turpentine.

Acrylic paint can be diluted with various liquids, or *media*, to give different effects. It can be thinned with water, but you can also buy a medium to slow down the drying time of the paint. Other media create a gloss or matte effect.

Cleaning up

After using water-soluble paints (including acrylic), brushes should be rinsed in water immediately. Smooth the hairs of your brushes back into shape and stand them bristles up to dry.

After using oils, brushes should be wiped on a rag or newspaper to remove excess paint. They should be cleaned first with turpentine and then with soap and water.

Put your oil painting somewhere safe to dry, which may take several months. When it is dry, you can paint it with a coat of varnish to protect it and give it a glossy surface.

INDEX

▽ *"This fishing village was painted in acrylic on board. Part of this large painting might work equally well on its own, or there could even be several paintings here. The L-shapes described on page 30 could be used to find out which parts work best."*

PRINTED IN BELGIUM BY

INTERNATIONAL BOOK PRODUCTION